Magic Tricks
YOU CAN DO!

Written by Robyn Supraner Illustrated by Renzo Barto

**Troll
Associates**

Library of Congress Cataloging in Publication Data

Supraner, Robyn.
    Magic tricks you can do!

    SUMMARY: Sheldon and Rosie demonstrate a variety
of simple and amusing magic tricks.
    1. Tricks—Juvenile literature.   2. Conjuring—
Juvenile literature.   [1. Magic tricks]   I. Barto,
Renzo.   II. Title.
GV1548.S96   793.8   80-19780
ISBN 0-89375-418-8
ISBN 0-89375-419-6 (pbk.)   AACR1

CONTENTS

"There is nothing to do," said Rosie.

"We could put on a magic show," said Sheldon. "I will be the magician. You can be my helper."

"Wrong," said Rosie. "I will be the magician. *You* can be my helper."

"It's my idea," complained Sheldon.

"It's my house!" said Rosie.

Sheldon thought about it. "We could take turns," he said. "I will go first."

"Be my guest," said Rosie. *"Abracadabra! Presto! Let the magic begin!"*

THE MAGIC CIRCLES

Sheldon put three paper circles on the back of his hand. "Watch very carefully," he said. He blew on the circles. They floated to the floor. "I am picking up the circles," said Sheldon. "I am putting them back on my hand."

"Big deal," said Rosie. "Anyone can do that."

Sheldon ignored her. "When I blow on my hand this time," he said, "only *two* circles will fly away. The other circle will not move."

"Really?" said Rosie.
"Really," said Sheldon. "You pick the circle. Pick any one."
"I pick the red one," said Rosie.
Magicadabra, magicaroo. I can do anything better than you!
said Sheldon.

He took a deep breath. Then he put his index finger on the red circle, and blew as hard as he could. The yellow and blue circles flew off his hand. The red circle did not move.

"You tricked me!" said Rosie.

"That's the way the cookie crumbles," said Sheldon.

THE MAGIC PAPER

"Here is a sheet of magic paper," said Rosie. "If you can tear it into four equal pieces, I will give you a quarter."

"That's easy," said Sheldon. He took the paper and folded it in half. He folded it in half again. Then he tore the paper along the folds.

"Here are your four equal pieces," said Sheldon.

"And here is your quarter," said Rosie. She handed him one of the squares.

"You tricked me!" said Sheldon.

"That's the way the ball bounces," said Rosie.

THE MAGIC TULIP

Sheldon put two pieces of white paper on a table. He put them under a bright light. On one, he drew a tulip. He colored the petals green. He colored the leaves red.

"That's a silly looking tulip," said Rosie.

"It's a magic tulip," said Sheldon. "If you stare at it and count to twenty-five, it will appear in its true colors on the other piece of paper."

Rosie stared at the tulip. She counted slowly to twenty-five. Then she looked at the blank piece of paper.

"I see it!" she said. "I see a red tulip with green leaves!"

"Don't applaud," said Sheldon. "Throw money!"

THE MAGIC DOLLAR

"I have a magic dollar," said Rosie. "I will drop it between your fingers. If you catch it, you can keep it."

"That's nice of you," said Sheldon.

"We will see," smiled Rosie. "Rest your arm on the table with your hand sticking over the edge. Hold your thumb away from your palm."

Sheldon did it.

Rosie put the dollar right in Sheldon's open hand. She held it between his thumb and fingers.

"Keep your eye on the dollar, and don't move your arm," she said. She let go of the dollar. Sheldon tried to grab it. The dollar fell to the floor.

"Try it again," said Sheldon.

They tried it again and again. Sheldon could not catch the dollar.

"It's amazing," said Sheldon.

"It's magic!" said Rosie.

THE MAGIC NAPKIN

"How strong are you?" asked Sheldon.

"They don't call me 'Rosie the Rock' for nothing," said Rosie.

Sheldon twisted a paper napkin until it looked like a rope. "You are not strong enough to tear this napkin," he said.

"Ha!" said Rosie. "Anyone can tear a napkin."

"Not this napkin," said Sheldon. "It's magic. You must try to tear it in half by pulling on both ends."

Rosie pulled the napkin. She pulled as hard as she could. "I can't budge it," she said.

"You could if you were a magician," said Sheldon. He took the napkin by its center, and held it above his head. *"Alacapudding. Alacapaff. Magic napkin, tear in half!"* he said. He pulled both ends of the napkin. It came apart easily.

"How did you do that?" asked Rosie.

"Magic water," said Sheldon.

"You wet it?" asked Rosie.

"I dipped my fingers in water when you weren't looking," said Sheldon. "It's easy to tear the napkin when the middle is just a little wet."

"You cheated!" said Rosie.

"Don't be bitter," said Sheldon.

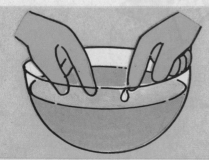

THE MAGIC PENNY

"Look through this cup," said Rosie. "What do you see?"

"I see a penny," said Sheldon.

"When I say the magic word, the penny will disappear," said Rosie. "I will now say the magic word. *Fleegle!*"

Rosie whisked the cup away.

"The penny is gone!" said Sheldon.

"*Fleegle* is a very magic word," said Rosie.

Here's what Rosie did:

1 Before she started her trick, she cut off the bottom of a paper cup.

2 She placed the cup on a piece of green paper and traced around it with a pencil. Then she cut out the circle.

3 She put some glue all around the rim of the cup and stuck the green circle to it. Then she let it dry. She trimmed the green paper around the cup.

4 She cut a mat from the piece of green paper and stood the paper cup on it.

5 Then she dropped a penny in the cup. When Sheldon looked at the penny, it only seemed to be lying on the green paper mat. It was really inside the paper cup.

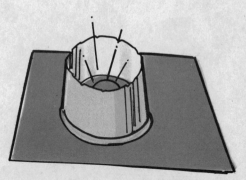

THE MAGIC MESSAGE

"Write a secret message on this piece of paper," said Sheldon. "Do not show the message to me."

Rosie wrote on the paper. Sheldon turned his back so he could not see what Rosie wrote.

"Now put the paper on the floor, and stand on it," said Sheldon.

Rosie stood on the paper. Only one little corner stuck out.

Sheldon put his fingers to his forehead. "I cannot see the message, but I know what is on the paper," he said.

"You do not," said Rosie.

"Magicians know everything," said Sheldon.

"All right," said Rosie. "If you're so smart, tell me what is on the paper."

"Your foot!" said Sheldon.

"You tricked me again!" said Rosie.

"Sorry about that," said Sheldon.

THE MAGIC GOLDFISH

Rosie drew a goldfish on a piece of white cardboard. She drew a fish bowl on the other side. Then she folded the sheet in half.

Rosie then taped a pencil inside the folded sheet. She taped the open end of the sheet to the other half of it.

"I am going to make the goldfish jump into the bowl," she said.

"Impossible!" said Sheldon.

"Magic!" said Rosie.

She rolled the pencil between her palms. She rolled it quickly.

"*Alacaboo! Alacabump! Jump, little goldfish! Jump! Jump! Jump!*" she said.

"You did it!" said Sheldon. "The goldfish is in the bowl!"

"It looks that way, doesn't it?" said Rosie.

THE MAGIC EGG

"I am going to spin this magic egg," said Sheldon. "When I touch it, it will stop. When I let go, it will spin again."

"If you drop it, you mop it," said Rosie.

"Eggy, weggy, geggy, meggy," said Sheldon.

"I beg your pardon?" asked Rosie.

"Stop interrupting," said Sheldon. "I am saying the magic words."

He gave the raw egg a good, hard spin. Then he stopped it with one finger.
When he lifted his finger, the egg began to spin again!

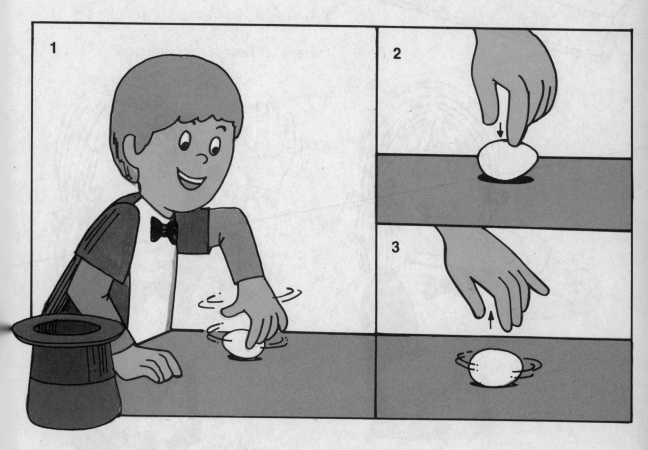

"That's a very good trick," said Rosie. "I wish that I could do it."

"You can," said Sheldon, "if you spin the egg hard enough and say the
magic words."

THE ENCHANTED FLOWER

"This is an enchanted flower," said Rosie. "It will grow when I say the magic words."

"It looks like a paper flower stuck to the end of a ruler," said Sheldon.

"You have no imagination," said Rosie.

"I see what I see," said Sheldon.

Rosie pushed the "stem" of the flower into her closed hand. She waved her other hand in the air. *"Hiffle, piffle. Sun or snow. Magic flower, grow, grow, grow!"* she said. The flower grew and grew.

"That's very good," said Sheldon. "How did you do it?"

"Don't ask," said Rosie. "I'll never tell."

Here's what Rosie did:

Before starting her trick, Rosie slipped a rubber band over her middle finger. When she pushed the flower into her hand, she stretched the rubber band. Then she opened her hand (just a little bit), and the rubber band pulled the flower up!

THE MAGIC BALLOON

"This may look like an ordinary balloon," said Sheldon.

"It certainly does," said Rosie.

"That is where you are wrong," said Sheldon. "What happens when you stick a pin in an ordinary balloon?"

"Ordinarily," said Rosie, "it pops."

"Correct," said Sheldon. "Now watch carefully. I am going to stick a pin in this balloon."
"It didn't pop!" said Rosie.

"Naturally," said Sheldon. "It is a magic balloon."
"It is?" said Rosie.
"It is," said Sheldon. He stuck another pin in the balloon.
"I like that trick," said Rosie. "How did you do it?"
"Don't ask," said Sheldon.
"I know," said Rosie. "You'll never tell."

Here's what Sheldon did:

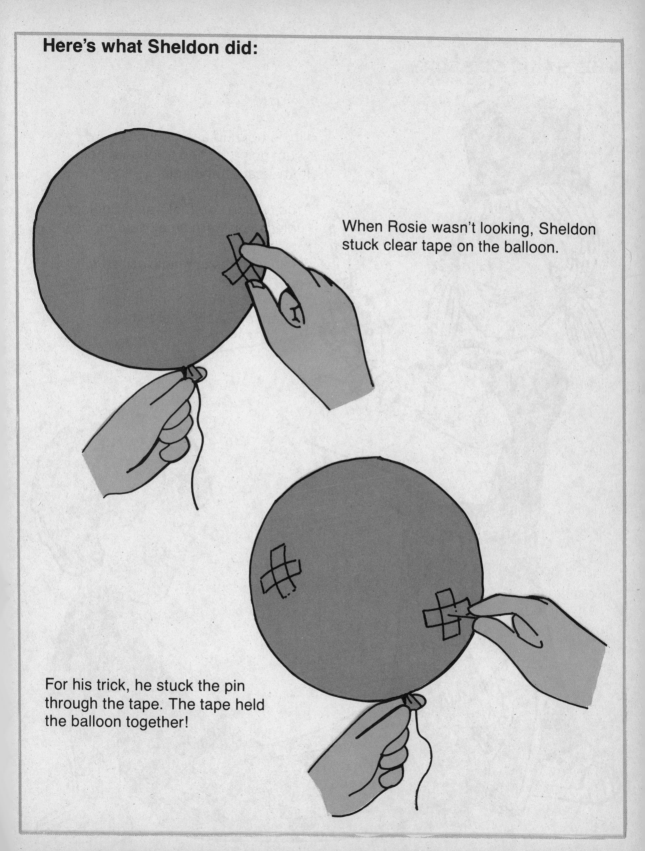

When Rosie wasn't looking, Sheldon stuck clear tape on the balloon.

For his trick, he stuck the pin through the tape. The tape held the balloon together!

THE MAGIC SCISSORS

Rosie held up a large index card. "I am going to step through a hole in this card," she said.

"You couldn't do that," said Sheldon, "unless you were small as a mouse."

"I can with these magic scissors," said Rosie.

"Dream on," said Sheldon.

Rosie folded the card in half, lengthwise.

She said, *"Magic scissors that I see, cut a giant hole for me!"*

Then she cut the card like this: she cut along the red lines. Then she turned the card around and cut along the blue lines. She cut along the fold line from A to B. When she was finished, she opened the card. She opened it slowly and carefully.

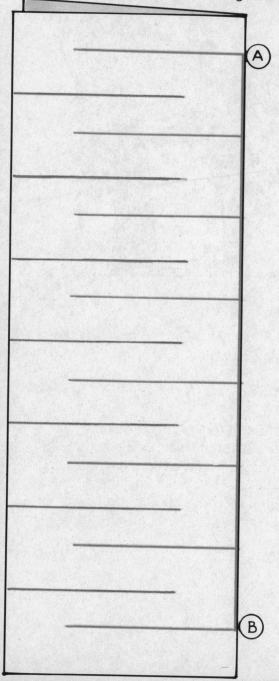

"I don't believe it!" said Sheldon.

"I thought you believed in magic," said Rosie, and she stepped through the hole in the card.

THE MAGIC POST CARD

"You are looking at a magic post card," said Sheldon.

"I am looking at a magic post card," said Rosie.

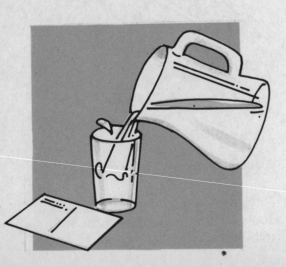

"Don't fool around," said Sheldon. "This post card is really magic." He filled a glass with water. He filled it until there was not room for another drop.

Then he held the post card over the mouth of the glass and quickly turned the glass upside down.

"When I take my hand away," he said, "the water will not fall out."

"I'll get my raincoat," said Rosie.

Sheldon took his hand away. The magic post card did not move! The water did not fall out!

"I like that trick!" said Rosie.

THE MAGIC HAT

Rosie held a top hat above her head. "This is my magic hat," she said.

"Good. If you put it on, will you disappear?" asked Sheldon.

"Very funny. Now, let's see if you can balance the hat on this single sheet of paper," said Rosie.

"Impossible. The hat's too heavy. The paper keeps caving in," said Sheldon.

"Allow me," said Rosie. "It's really quite simple. This is what you do."

Rosie folded the paper like an accordion. She stood it on the table. Then she placed the top hat on the pleated sheet.

THE MAGIC TUBE

Sheldon had two cardboard tubes. He gave one to Rosie.

"Hold your tube on the table like this," he said.

Rosie did it.

"Now lift your hand," said Sheldon.

Rosie lifted her hand. The tube fell on the floor.

"Oops!" said Sheldon. "I forgot to tell you the magic word."

"What magic word?" asked Rosie.

"Floogle!" said Sheldon. He lifted his hand. The tube did not fall!

"What kept it from falling?" asked Rosie.

"Floogle," said Sheldon. "What else?"

Here's what Sheldon did:

He stuffed a lump of clay into one end of his tube. He rested the heavy end of the tube on the table. The extra weight kept it from falling off. *Note:* When no one is looking, test this trick first. If you need more clay, add it.

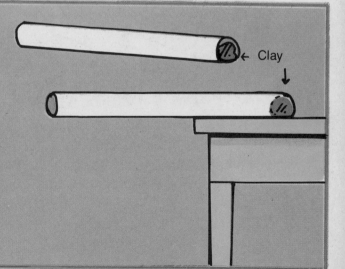

← Clay

THE MAGIC ENVELOPE

Rosie asked Sheldon to write down the name of any president of the United States.

She waved an envelope in the air. "This is a magic envelope," she said. "When I open it, you will see that I have already written down that name."

"I will pick a hard name," said Sheldon. He thought and thought. Then he wrote "Zachary Taylor." "There!" he said. "I bet you don't have that name."

"I bet I do," said Rosie. She tore open the magic envelope.

"You tricked me!" said Sheldon.

"That's true!" laughed Rosie.

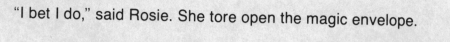

TRICKY CURVES

"I will place one curve above the other," said Sheldon.
"Now tell me which curve is shorter."

"That's easy," said Rosie. "The top one is shorter."

"All right," said Sheldon, "I will attempt to stretch the top curve so they will both be the same size."

Sheldon tugged at each end of the curve and then placed it below the other curve.

"Hold it!" said Rosie. "Now it's longer than the other curve."

"Let me check this out," said Sheldon. He picked up both curves and placed one over the other. "Look, they're the same size," he said.

"That's strange!" said Rosie.

"That's the way the curve bends!" said Sheldon.

Here's what Sheldon did:

Using two sheets of construction paper, he cut two copies of this shape out of brightly colored construction paper.

From darker construction paper, he cut out two copies of this shape. Then he glued the smaller pieces to the bottom of each of the larger pieces.

Note: When doing this trick, set up the two curves as shown here. After "tugging" on the top one, be sure to place it below the other curve.

THE MAGIC CLIPS

"I have two magic paper clips," said Rosie. "When I place them on this paper and say the magic words, they will become joined together."

"This I have to see to believe," said Sheldon.

Rosie bent the paper and put the clips on it like this.

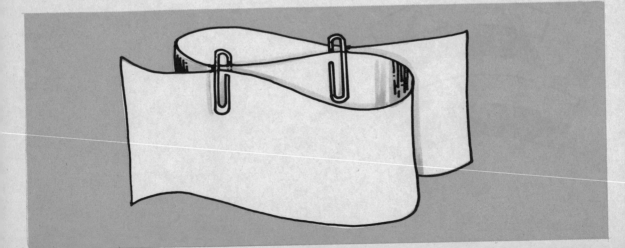

"O.K., here goes," said Rosie. *"Razzle, dazzle, deezle, dips! Fly together, paper clips!"* She tugged sharply at each end of the paper. The clips flew up in the air. When they landed, they were clipped together.

"Look at that," said Sheldon. "That's real magic!"

"Anyone can do it," said Rosie, "if they say the magic words."

THE MAGIC SPELLING CARDS

"Here's a card trick for you," said Sheldon.

"Great," said Rosie, "I love card tricks."

"I have thirteen cards from Ace all the way to King," began Sheldon. "As you can see, they're all mixed up. I'll keep them face down. Starting with Ace, I'll spell out the name of each card. A-C-E. For each letter, I'll put the card on top of the deck on the bottom. When I'm finished spelling, the next card I turn over will be the one I've just spelled. Then I'll take the card I've just spelled out of the deck. We'll start with Ace and go in numerical order up to Ten, Jack, Queen, King."

"Wow, let's get going," said Rosie. Sheldon spelled out each card, all the way to King, and it worked!

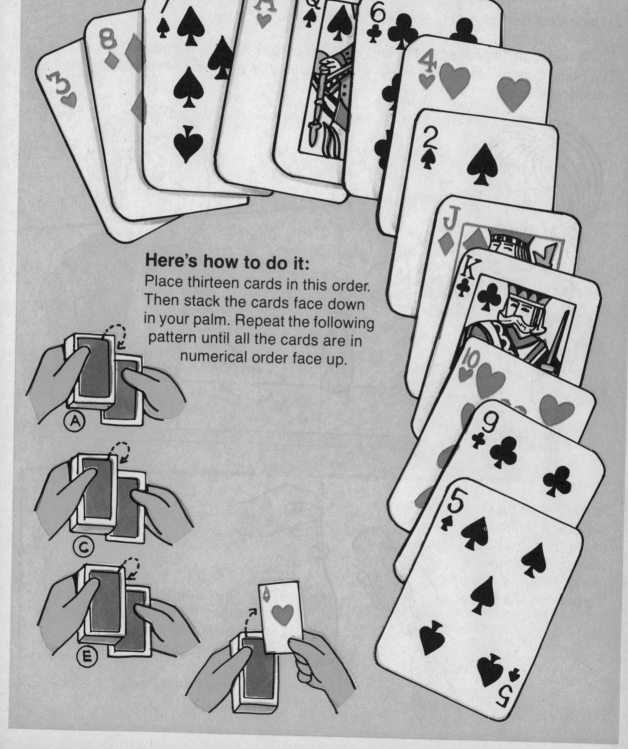

Here's how to do it:

Place thirteen cards in this order. Then stack the cards face down in your palm. Repeat the following pattern until all the cards are in numerical order face up.

THE MAGIC BOTTLE

"With this special rope," said Rosie, "I will lift this magic bottle into the air."

"I hope your bottle is unbreakable!" said Sheldon.

Rosie had a small-necked bottle and a length of rope about 8-inches long. The bottle was painted solid red. (A plastic bottle that you can't see through can also be used.)

Rosie picked up the bottle and put the end of the rope in it. "Just want to make sure there isn't any water in the bottle," said Rosie.

Then she turned the bottle right side up, holding only the rope. "Wow! The rope is really holding up the bottle," said Sheldon.

"Of course," said Rosie, "this is a magic bottle!"

Here's how Rosie did it:

Rosie made a small ball of clay, just large enough to fit into the bottle. She kept the clay ball hidden in the palm of her hand. As she picked the bottle up, she slipped the ball into the bottle. She then tipped the bottle sideways to let the ball roll up to the bottle's neck, tugging on the rope lightly to lock the rope into place. Then she turned the bottle right side up, holding it by the rope.

To release the rope, Rosie turned the bottle sideways. She pushed the rope into the bottle about an inch and pulled out the rope.

Sheldon placed a dime and a quarter, touching each other, on a table. Putting a penny on the table, he asked Rosie, "Can you put this penny in between the dime and quarter?"

"That's easy," said Rosie. She pushed the dime over a bit and slid the penny in between.

"Hold it!" said Sheldon. "There are a few rules I haven't told you yet."

"O.K.," said Rosie. "Tell me."

1. The dime can be moved, but cannot be touched by hand or with the penny.

2. The quarter can be touched by hand, but it cannot be moved.

3. The penny can be moved by hand. None of the coins can be picked up.

"There is no way to do it," said Rosie.

"Just to show you that the quarter does not move," said Sheldon, "hold the quarter down with your index finger." Rosie held the quarter down. Sheldon put his finger on the penny and flicked it sharply against the quarter.

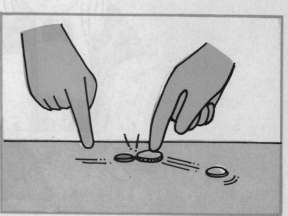

The quarter never budged, but the dime moved away from the quarter.

"Now," said Sheldon, "I will simply slide the penny between the quarter and dime."

"Why did that happen?" asked Rosie.

"It's a magical force," said Sheldon.

"You are a tricky magician," said Rosie.

"Well, so are you," said Sheldon. "Let's call our magic show *The Tricky Magicians!*"

Date Due

2-27-00		
8-30-07		
8-30-12		

Code 4386-04, CLS-4, Broadman Supplies, Nashville, Tenn.,
Printed in U.S.A.